A Very Special Gift Book

of

Winning Thoughts

Carl Mays

The Lincoln-Bradley Publishing Group

New York

Memphis   *Gatlinburg*

Produced in conjunction with
The Alice Moore Gallery
Gatlinburg, Tennessee

Inquiries should be addressed to:

The Lincoln-Bradley Publishing Group
c/o Creative Living, Inc.
P.O. Box 808
Gatlinburg, Tennessee 37738

(615) 436-4150

Publisher's Cataloging in Publication

Mays, Carl
    Winning thoughts / by Carl Mays
        p. cm.
    ISBN 1-879111-23-3
    1. Winning - Quotations, maxims, etc.
2. Success - Quotations, maxims, etc.
3. Conduct of life - Quotations, maxims,
etc. I. Title.
BJ1482.3   1994   819.'5401

Book Design & Make-up by
Electronic Publishing Services, Inc.
Type Face: Novarese

1 2 3 4 5 6 7 8 9 10

Introduction

As a professional speaker and writer since the mid-seventies, specializing in motivation, performance improvement and human relations, I have had the opportunity to work with many organizations.

Through the years, the corporations, sports teams and family groups with whom I have worked, have asked me to address certain situations and specific obstacles they were facing. As a result, I have written quotes, verses and brief maxims to share with them. These, along with new writings presented here for the first time, are the "Winning Thoughts" I now offer you in this gift book.

I have been told that many of these ideas have been instrumental in corporations improving, sports teams winning and families reuniting. It is my hope that they might make a positive difference in your life or in the life of someone important to you.

— Carl Mays
Gatlinburg, Tennessee

For Jean, my wife.

I *count as joy*
our days together.
I *count as pleasure*
the work we've done.

Through all the challenges
of our tasks,
I *count the efforts*
rewarding fun.

CONTENTS

A Strategy For Winning

Several of the writings in this gift book have been adapted from **A Strategy For Winning** (ISBN 1-879111-75-6), the 272-page hardcover book ($21.95) written by Carl Mays and published by *Lincoln-Bradley*. The adaptations are used with permission and are indicated herein with asterisks (* *).

To obtain a copy of **A Strategy For Winning,** please check with your local bookstore. Or, you may phone the publisher at 1-800-I CAN WIN (422-6946).

Principle Number One

in

* A Strategy For Winning *

Accept Yourself And Your Worth

Appreciate who you are.

Get to know yourself better.

We all have strengths and weaknesses. What we do with them is the important thing. Discover, develop and use your strengths wisely. Utilize them to help you to improve in your areas of weakness.

Your self-image determines how you will live your life. It determines how you will perform in your career. It determines how you will perform as a wife, a husband, a parent, a student, an athlete and a member of society.

BELIEVE in yourself!

* Only One You *

In the history of the world, there has been only one you. There will never be anyone else exactly like you.

If you don't develop what you have, the world will never experience an individual who can do exactly what you can do, the way you can do it — in family, in career, in sports, in school and in society.

The victories, the completeness, the success and the lifestyle that you can achieve, is only for you. It's not for anyone else. And you deserve to be the best that you can possibly be!

Believe!

Success
is hard to find
in the lives of people
who doubt they can achieve
it.

Be You

Drama, music, sports?

Maybe business, math or art?

What are your talents, likes — dislikes?

How can you do your part?

Teaching, writing, medicine?

Helping others who have lost the way?

Finding a niche and doing your thing...

This makes a happy day!

Inner Power

God
has
given
you
the
power
to
match
your
dreams
with
reality.
Use
it!

* Sing Your Song! *

Individually, we average hearing seven criticisms to every one compliment. And most of us remember the negative comments far longer than the positive statements.

As we often see ourselves through the eyes of people who discourage us, many of our limitations become self-imposed. This is why Oliver Wendell Holmes wrote:

"Most of us die
with our music still in us."

I challenge you to remove those self-imposed limitations. I challenge you to release your music. I challenge you to SING YOUR SONG!

12

God Knows Better...

Do not

accept someone

else's low opinion of you.

God knows better — and you should too!

Winners

Winners control their destiny.
Winners take a stand.
Winners make things happen.
Winners say, "I *can!*"

Winners don't make excuses.
Winners do what they can do.
Winners are responsible.
Winners carry through.

Winners win with class.
Winners lose with grace.
Winners hold their heads up high.
Winners look you in the face.

Winners' deeds tell the story.
Winners act more than talk.
Winners win with dignity.
Winners walk the walk.

To Be A Champion

THINK like a Champion.

TALK like a Champion.

LOOK like a Champion.

ACT like a Champion.

PERFORM like a Champion!

Satisfaction

Satisfaction...

is knowing
you have done your best
to become
the best you can become.

Principle Number Two

in

* A Strategy For Winning *

Develop And Maintain A Winning Attitude

Problems can bring out the worst or best in you.

You can fold under pressure or you can tap powerful resources that are already within you, to help you become stronger rather than weaker.

The way you think, changes the way you look and perform.

Many people hope and wish to win, but never raise their confidence levels high enough to really EXPECT to win.

Do your homework. Be prepared. Then step out — with GREAT EXPECTATIONS!

* Obstacle or Opportunity? *

Often, the main difference between
an obstacle and an opportunity
is the attitude with which we face it.

_____

Are you pinned-in on your one-yard line?

OR

Do you have a great opportunity
to go 99 yards for a touchdown!

Expectations

If you expect to lose,
      that's what you choose,
            and the odds are high that you will.

If you expect to win,
      your mind's your friend;
            your thoughts can make it real.

As you enter the fight,
      get your mind right,
            to create a winning condition.

The way you go in,
      can lead to a win,
            and establish a winning tradition!

* Look For Ways To Win *

Mahatma Ghandi said:

> If I *believe I cannot do some-*
> *thing, it makes me incapable of*
> *doing it. But when I believe I*
> *can, then I acquire the ability to*
> *do it, even if I did not have the*
> *ability in the beginning.*

You shouldn't close your eyes to problems or obstacles; you should be realistic. But, at the same time...

Look For Ways To Win
rather than
Excuses For Losing!

* Don't Wait! *

Most people
develop feelings
as a result of happenings;
winners develop happenings
as a result of feelings.

BELIEVE that you can make a positive difference.
WORK to make it happen.

Losers find ways to lose
while
Winners find ways to WIN!

Faith

Frustration.
This is common
in the life of many.
A chronic disease in the land of plenty.

Faith.
This is the antidote
that will bring you through.
Faith in God and faith in you!

Create Conditions

Dream

Hope   Pray

Work   Believe   Expect

and

You will create conditions

in which

good things can happen!

A–T–T–I–T–U–D–E

A - Attempt

T - The

T - Things

I - Impossible

T - To

U - Uninspired

D - Defeated

E - Excuses

The Winner

When you're counted out,
do you give up the bout?
Do you accept their decision
and fall?

When they say you're through,
what do you do?
Do you work harder
to win it all?

It's easy to say,
"this is just not my day."
It's easy to fold up
and leave.

But the winner hangs tough
when the going is rough.
The winner works — and says,
"I BELIEVE!"

* C-L-A-S-S *

Practice with . . . . C - Commitment
L - Loyalty
A - Aggressiveness
S - Sincerity
S - Self-awareness

Perform with . . . . C - Certainty
L - Leadership
A - Abandon
S - Sharpness
S - Self-confidence

Win with . . . . C - Creativity
L - Love
A - Authority
S - Smartness
S - Self-control

Principle Number Three

in

* A Strategy For Winning *

Be Creative

Take an idea, an object, a group of people, a method, a problem — something that's been around awhile — stand back and look at it with a new perspective (*a fresh pair of eyes*). Give it a different twist.

Do

A *Common Thing*

Uncommonly

Well!

* What If? *

In 1901, H.C. Booth was sitting in a rocking chair on his front porch, watching the sun set. He was also watching the dust blow across the prairie.

As he relaxed and rocked, he asked himself, "What if we could reverse that wind and pull the dust rather than blow it?"

H.C. Booth invented the vacuum cleaner.

Have you asked, "What if?" lately?

"What if we tried it this way?"

"What if we changed that procedure?"

"What if I changed my lifestyle?"

"What if I changed my attitude?"

"WHAT IF?"

To Really Live

To really live is

    to be curious,

        to wonder,

           to dream,

               to be surprised

                   by simple things.

Thank God for Problems!

Problems
stimulate creativity.

Creativity
leads to solutions.

Solutions
lead to change.

Change
leads to challenge and growth!

* To Be Creative When Problems Arise *

- Admit the problem.

- Define the problem.

- Gather resources.

- Consider various possibilities.

- Mull it over.

- Choose the best solution.

- Try it out.

The Child

Recapture
the little child
in you;
the one that was there
before
you learned
what you couldn't do.

Get On Top of Your Problem

When you have a problem,
climb up above it
and look down
upon it.

Look at the problem
with fresh eyes
and give it a
different twist.

See what you have never
seen before.
Creative ideas
will come.

With a new sense of power,
you can solve what's
below you
from within.

Are You A Leader?

When the game's on the line
and you're about out of time
and things are not going your way,
can you reach down inside,
can you find that pride,
can you step forward
and make the play?

When others give up
and curse their luck
and you see them hang their head,
do you have what it takes
to make your own breaks,
can you bring them back
from the dead?

It's easy to smile
when you're ahead by a mile,
it's easy to laugh and joke,
but when you're behind
that's when you'll find
you'll rise to the top
or choke.

How To Win

- Know What You Are Doing.

- Believe In What You Are Doing.

- Practice Doing What You Want To Do.

- Stop Worrying.

- Create Opportunities.

- Stop Talking And Start Doing.

- Don't Quit.

* The Difference *

Attention
to
the little details
is what often separates the champion
and
the near champion.

Principle Number Four

in

* A Strategy For Winning *

Don't Fear Failure

There's a big difference between temporary failure and total defeat.

Many of our successes are built upon what we learn from our failures. People who resist all forms of failure rarely succeed. People whose main purpose in life is to play it safe rarely expand.

Don't Be Afraid Of Life!

****

Don't Miss Smelling The Flowers

For Fear

You May Get Stung By A Bee!

****

Focus On Today

Move away from your past failures.

Forget your past mistakes.

Focus on today.

That's what winning takes.

       Yesterday is over.

       Today is important now.

       Work toward current goals.

       Concentrate on **HOW!**

* Keep On Keeping On *

When you are through
learning,
growing,
improving,
you are through.

– So –

KEEP ON KEEPING ON!

* The Three "R's" *

Being "down but not out" is one of the greatest attributes one can possess.

Overcoming seemingly insurmountable odds to taste the sweetness of victory is one of the greatest feelings one can experience.

Three keys to being

... "down but not out" ...

- *Be Receptive.*

  Face up to the adversity.

- *Be Resourceful.*

  Discover, develop, use your strengths.

- *Be Resurgent.*

  Rise again — and again — and again...

Stay

It's easy to give up
when the going is rough.
It's easy to hang your head.

But to carry the load
when others won't,
that's the challenge instead.

As you fight against hope
and your chances are slim,
it would be easy to crawl away.

But hold your head high.
It's not time to die.
Now is the time to STAY!

* Victory *

Controlled Emotion, Focused Energy

and

Unbelievable Persistence

Lead to VICTORY!

Beethoven rose above deafness to compose majestic music.

Helen Keller, who could neither see, hear, nor speak for a long time, carved an indelible place in history.

Louisa Mae Alcott was told by an editor that she had no writing ability and should forget about attempting it. *Little Women* came shortly thereafter.

When Walt Disney submitted his first drawings for publication, the editor told him he had no talent — especially when it came to drawing small animals!

We can learn from these people!

Formula For Success

$$(1\,T + 4\,D = S)$$

Talent
+ Desire
+ Dedication
+ Discipline
+ Determination
_____
SUCCESS

After We Know It All

The things that help us to win...

the things that lead to the top...

the things that keep us going...

when we really want to stop...

the things that pick us up...

after a crushing fall...

are all those things we learn...

after we know it all!

Accept Responsibility

Mistakes

become defeats

when

we start blaming someone else.

Take A Winner's Stand!

Never say,
"It *can't be done.*"

Declare,
"*Indeed, it can!*"

Then,
do the things you need to do
to
TAKE A WINNER'S STAND!

Principle Number Five

in

* A Strategy For Winning *

Clarify Your Values

Act rather than react. When you adhere to a set system of values, you will discover more productivity, harmony, fulfillment and profitability in all areas of life.

Our challenge is to clarify moral values, spiritual values and relationship values.

Some people are **THERMOSTATS**. These people set the temperature; these people take the initiative.

Some people are **THERMOMETERS**. These people simply react and record the temperature set by others; these people respond to others' standards.

Which are you?

Read on!

Give Me The Courage

Give me the courage
to be my own person.

Give me the courage
to take a stand.

Give me the courage
to live for a purpose.

Give me the courage
to do what I can.

Give me the courage
to make a difference.

Give me the courage
to know why I'm here.

Give me the courage
to step out on faith.

Give me the courage
to overcome fear!

Peace Is A Mountain Top Experience

Peace is more than a season...
it is a way of thinking,
a way of being,
an inner security
unaffected by outward things.

Peace is a mountain top experience...
may you scale the heights,
find the treasure
and share it with others.

* Plant A Tree *

An elderly man was planting a small apple tree. A younger man said, "Why are you planting that? You'll be dead before it bears fruit."

The elderly man answered, "Son, everything is not just for ourselves."

Give

If you want to be a better person
tomorrow than you were today,
do something for someone
without expecting
anything in
return.

What About Just Being Nice?

We have seminars on customer service,
time management,
QUAL-I-TY.

We have seminars on sales and marketing,
handling change
as the KEY.

But what about being kind and gentle,
being tolerant
once or TWICE?

What about being polite and thoughtful —
what about just
being NICE?

* GROWTH *

There are two ways a person can grow in his or her mind.

First, the person can seem to appear larger by making other people appear smaller.

Secondly, the person can actually grow by concentrating upon and developing what he or she has and by helping others to do the same.

The second method of growth leads to greater happiness and success in life.

Friends

The world at large
is full of challenges,
with various means
to an end.

And in this world
of so many challenges,
I am thankful for
my friends!

The Old Cracker Barrel

"I remember *The Old Cracker Barrel,*"
the elderly man told me.

"We'd sit around and swap our stories,
and sip our coffee or tea.

"We learned a lot just listening...
It's amazing what you can hear.

"The best tool for education?
...an open mind and an open ear."

Do You Know What You Have?

When
you
find
happiness,

be
sure
to
stop
and
enjoy
it,

or
you
might
never
KNOW
you
had
it!

Principle Number Six

in

* A Strategy For Winning *

Set Goals

The one purpose of goal-setting is to help you accomplish what you want to accomplish in all areas of life. Setting, planning and working toward clear, specific goals will lead you to the winner's circle, if you never, never, never give up...

You

may compete

against someone more talented than you,

but never allow yourself to compete

against someone more prepared!

* Scientific Goal Setting *

- Set specific goals.

- Don't set goals too low or too high.

- Put your goals in writing.

- Develop a plan; determine a deadline.

- Develop a sincere desire.

- Don't take your eyes off your goals.

- Concentrate upon the task at hand.

G-O-A-L-S

G – Get goals etched in your mind.

O – Organize your plans to reach them.

A – Accomplish plans step by step.

L – Leave nothing to chance.

S – Succeed with perseverance.

Hold On!

A dream is worth a fortune
Hold On To It!

A dream is bright and exciting
Hold On To It!

A dream multiplies the spirit
Hold On To It!

A dream magnifies even the simplest joys
Hold On To It!

A dream is the possession of a lucky few
Hold On To It!

A dream is like a kite on a taut string
Hold On To It!

Decisions

What must I give up
in order to get
what I want?

What am I willing
to sacrifice
to reach my goals?

What must I postpone today
to receive what I desire
tomorrow?

My major decisions in life
are not in choosing between
the *good* and the *bad*.

My major decisions
are choosing from among
the *good*, the *better* and the *best*.

What Can I Do?

What can I do

this year

this month

this week

today

NOW

that would have the greatest impact

upon

my long-term goals?

* Choices *

To

have

sufficient time

for the things that count,

we must eliminate the things that do not

count!

* Realize Your Potential *

With organization

and planned procedures

toward a realistic goal,

you can realize

a large percentage

of your potential!

YOU Are The Carpenter

When you get down to the nitty-gritty,

after all is said and done,

life is a frame of mind.

It is your life.

It is your frame.

YOU are the carpenter!

Do It!

Say you can.

Form your plan.

Plan your work.

Be alert.

Do it!

Principle Number Seven

in

* A Strategy For Winning *

Visualize

Visualization is seeing things happen before they actually happen, then doing the things that need to be done to make them come true.

Simply put, visualization is *"making pictures in your mind."*

Getting a vision and keeping it steadfast in your mind will help you do the things you need to do in order to make the vision materialize.

Through the visualization technique, I helped a major college basketball team increase its free throw shooting percentage from around 50% to 87%!

Again using visualization, I helped a sales organization increase their sales by 300% in one year!

All areas of our lives can benefit from visualization. It is *"mental engineering"* at its best!

* He Had "Been There" *

When Neil Armstrong stepped out onto the moon and then returned to earth, a reporter asked him, "What did it feel like?"

"It felt like I had been there 1,000 times before," the astronaut replied.

He had done it so many times in his mind, that when it actually happened, it wasn't new.

You can have the same feeling when your visualizations come true.

* See It *

Those who can see the invisible can do the impossible!

Disney World was not completed until after the death of Walt Disney. Shortly following the theme park's opening, a person who was touring the facility remarked to his host, "Isn't it a shame that Walt did not live to see this wonderful park?"

The host replied, "He did see it. That's why it is here today!"

* How To Visualize *

- Determine, in detail, exactly what you want to visualize.

- Believe it will make a positive difference in your life.

- Relax. If possible, lie down and close your eyes.

- Experience the visualization with as many of the five senses as possible.

- Be enthusiastic. Get "caught up" in your visualization experience.

- Visualize as often as you can, even when you can't lie down or close your eyes.

My Dreams

I can see my dreams.
I may never reach them all
but no one can take them from me.

I can see my dreams.
They give me joy and meaning
and purpose for being.

I can see my dreams.
I believe in them and
they help me to believe in me.

I Can See My Dreams.

Focus For Success

Like

a beam of sunlight shining

brilliantly through a magnifying glass,

focus your talents, abilities and desire

upon your dreams

and

never

never

never give up!

* Enthusiasm *

There is nothing quite like enthusiasm.

It brings
HOPE
where hope did not exist.

It turns on a
LIGHT
in the middle of darkness.

ENTHUSIASM
turns losers into
WINNERS!

Little by Little

When something appears overwhelming,
and there's no way to get it done,
reduce it to its smallest parts,
and take care of them,
one by
one
!

Where Are You?

ACTION comes before victory.

PLANS come before action.

GOALS come before plans.

VISIONS come before goals.

INSPIRATION comes before visions.

Where are YOU in THE PROCESS?

The Process

Feel It.

Dream It.

Plan It.

Pursue It.

Do It!

Principle Number Eight

in

* A Strategy For Winning *

Enjoy, Like And Appreciate Other People

- TEAMWORK -

Many corporations, sports teams and other organizations with talented individuals have never become winning groups because they can't live together, work together or win together.

In the end, success comes when people work successfully with people.

There is nothing as powerful and contagious as positive, uplifting enthusiasm that is handled wisely by a group of people who respect one another and contribute their individual talents and abilities, coming together as one united force to reach one common cause, goal or dream!

To Live Successfully

To live successfully,
one must overcome
his or her own difficulty
in dealing with people.

Everyone has done
and has said
the wrong things
at the wrong times.

Work to develop
a tactful and
skillful touch
in relating to others.

It doesn't just happen.
It comes with thought,
work and, most of all,
unselfishness.

Mutual Trust

Do I trust you?
Do you trust me?
Mutual Trust
leads to
VICTORY!

A Lesson From The Ants

Ants are...

ACTIVE with specific, purposeful tasks, doing the little things that must be done to accomplish impossible projects together.

DETERMINED. If they can't do the job alone, they call others to help, defying unthinkable odds to succeed.

SHARING in jobs, hardships, accomplishments and rewards, they live to help one another.

COOPERATIVE, accepting individual responsibility as they perform as a team, often sacrificing for the good of the group.

WISE, known for doing the most they can with what they have, they take full advantage of talents and abilities.

Amazing Results

It
is amazing
what people can do
when they work together!

Teamwork

The wisdom of *Ecclesiastes* is powerful and the lesson on teamwork is simple:

> *One standing alone can be attacked*
> *and defeated, but two can stand*
> *back-to-back and conquer; three is*
> *even better, for a triple-braided cord*
> *is not easily broken.*

Working together willingly for a common purpose can lead to the accomplishment of seemingly impossible tasks.

Think About It

What kind of team
would this
team be,
if everyone
thought,
acted,
performed,
just like
me?

Success Through Others

The better
I work with people,
the more successful
I become!

* Someone In Your Corner *

Be thankful for the people who help you to grow, who help you to become what you have the potential to become. You may not always agree with them, but it's great to know you have someone in your corner pulling for you, ready to help you when you fall and ready to cheer you when you succeed.

You should feel extremely fortunate to have someone who will stand with you and support you during the hard times as well as the good. Almost anyone will stick by you when things are alright; cherish the one who stays with you when things are not alright. Cherish the one who says, "I believe in you — right or wrong — I believe in you."

I Am Here

As you dream your dreams,
set your goals, make your plans
and take your steps,
I know you must have your solitude.

But if you need someone to
stand by you
and steady your arms
as you hold the world on your shoulders,
I *am here*.

Principle Number Nine

in

* A Strategy For Winning *

Do It Now!

Go For It!

To reach your goals in life, you have to take the offensive. You can't sit back and wait for things to happen. You have to make them happen. Many dreams never come true because of putting things off until "tomorrow."

* * * * * * * * *

If you get too caught up in thinking

about what you are going to do tomorrow

or about what you failed to do yesterday

you might not have time to do anything

today!

* * * * * * * * * * * * * * * * * *

* Do It Now! *

We Procrastinate Because...

- We are not prepared.
- We see something as being unpleasant, difficult or boring.
- We don't feel the problem is squeaking loudly enough yet.
- We don't have enough time to do it now.
- We allow other people to talk us into procrastinating.

We Can Overcome It By...

- Planning ahead.
- Making things creative or fun.
- Using preventive maintenance before the squeaking begins.
- Taking advantage of small bits of time.
- Being decisive.

T–O–D–A–Y

T – **Take** hold of today,

O – **Overcoming** adversity and

D – **Dedicating** yourself to a winning

A – **Attitude** that will carry

Y – **You** to the top!

Blaze A Trail

Some people
are always looking for
the well-worn path that will lead
to success, fulfillment and happiness.

Maybe there is no path
to where you want
to go.

Paths, like people,
are unique.

Paths which have led others to
their mountain tops,
may have been blazed by those people.

Take The Plunge!

While others
are standing on shore
waiting for their ships to come in,
TAKE THE PLUNGE
and
swim out to meet
YOURS!

One Of These Days...

One of these days,
I'm gonna' do this.

One of these days,
I'm gonna' do that.

One of these days,
I'll find the time.

One of these days,
I'll swing my bat.

But here I stand,
with good intentions.

Here I stand,
I'm growing older.

Pitches of life
pass by me quickly.

The bat I hold,
still on my shoulder.

Lesson: **SWING FOR THE BLEACHERS!**

* How Are You Doing? *

Are You Still Improving

or

Are You Still?

●

Move Out... Move On... Move Up...

to

HIGHER GROUND!

* A–C–T–I–O–N *

A – ATTACK the problems or obstacles that stand between you and your goals. Take the initiative.

C – CREATE opportunities. An ancient Chinese proverb says: *"One who waits for roast duck to fly into mouth must wait very, very long time."*

T – TOGETHERNESS turns the impossible into the possible. The total of an outstanding team is greater than its individual parts.

I – INSTILL a burning desire. Success is almost always dependent upon desire, drive and persistence.

O – OVERCOME adversity. You cannot become a true winner unless you can overcome adversity. The process makes you stronger.

N – NOW is the time to act. Putting off things destroys individuals and teams. **DO IT NOW!**

Stay Hungry And Lean

Don't rest on your victories
and be taken in;
don't become vulnerable
because of a win.

Keep the fire in your eyes,
stay hungry and lean;
satisfaction can dull
a well-oiled machine.

Never be satisfied and
say, "I've arrived."
Keep striving for more
and build on your pride.

What you did yesterday
is over and gone,
Your actions today
are what keep you strong.

May You

May you reach the goals
you've worked for.
May the things you've dreamed
come true.

May you help the lives
of many
in all you think and say
and do.